SANTA MARIA PUBLIC LIBRARY

ICEBERGS AND GLACIERS

Life at the Frozen Edge

Writer
Barbara Wilson

Series Editor
Vicki León

Principal Photographer
Art Wolfe

Additional Photographers

Tom Bean	Frans Lanting
Ralph A. Clevenger	Brian P. Lawler
Ken Cole	Tom Mangelsen
Jeff Foott	Kevin Schafer
John Fowler	Twila Stofer
François Gohier	Tim Thompson
Richard Hansen	Larry Ulrich
Fred Hirschmann	Kennan Ward

Designers
David Butz and Ashala Nicols-Lawler

BLAKE PUBLISHING
A GRAPHIC CENTER COMPANY

© 1990 Blake Publishing
2222 Beebee Street, San Luis Obispo, California 93401
All rights reserved. Printed in the United States of America
ISBN 0-918303-23-0

BIRTH OF A GLACIER

The story of glaciers and icebergs is a story of living things. Born in the vast silence of high snowfields, a glacier grows, changes, subsides, disappears. It is a story rich in clues, in buried mysteries much older than human memory. Massive ice sheets such as those in Antarctica are more than a million years old. Even "young" glaciers can date back to our most recent Ice Age, at its peak about 18,000 years ago.

Although people have long lived in the vicinity of glaciers, it is only in the last two centuries that we have begun to know much about them. Before the 1700s, there were only hints about the almost-mythic forces which had played out their stories in the fjords of Alaska, the scarred hills of Wisconsin, leaving their giant boulders stranded in the middle of Indiana plains, their claw marks scratched high in the alpine valleys of northern California. All over the world, the scars remain, older now, polished, still eloquent about the time when ice covered one-third of the world's surface.

So what are glaciers? How did these silent white beasts hidden in remote valleys cause the havoc they did? The Tlingit Indians of Southeast Alaska called them "ice mountains." From afar, they do look solid, like great frozen

Glaciers in your back yard. Folks in Juneau, Alaska, don't have far to look for glacial action. The white and pale blue mass of Mendenhall Glacier looms inside the city limits.

slabs pulling in light, holding the glow in millions of tiny prisms. They are, however, neither solid nor immovable. Glaciers are more like rivers of ice, vast moving systems of accumulation, compression, flow, and ablation.

A glacier is born high in the icy solitudes of snowfields. There snow accumulates winter after winter, the cold gray skies thick with flakes month after month, each one settling into last year's pack. In this accumulation zone, compacted granular snow piles up year after year. Because temperatures in high snowfields stay consistently low, the snow does not melt. Compacted snow more than a year old is called firn. The slowly accumulating weight of the firn squeezes air out of the snow layers. This action, combined with the slow refreezing of water trickling from warmer surface snow, turns the firn to ice.

A glacier, however, is not just compact snow that has turned to ice. If it were, anyone in northern cities could study glaciers on city sidewalks. What makes a glacier different is its movement. When the compact snow and firn reach a critical depth, a glacier begins to flow. It is hard to imagine tons of compacted ice oozing down mountain valleys. But that is exactly what it does. With enough weight on top, the underbelly of a glacier turns plastic, like pancake batter. It bends around obstacles, creating just enough friction to melt a bottom layer which serves as lubricant. River-like, most glaciers spill downward, at first taking on the valley's shape.

Fed at its upper end by snow and ice fields, a glacier carries ice along with chunks of

At far right, a good example of a tidal glacier in Alaska's Glacier Bay National Park. Where it touches the water, icebergs calve. You can gauge the height of the glacier by the size of the cruise ship it dwarfs. Below, a valley glacier whitens the flanks of Mt. Rainier near Seattle, Washington. Besides Rainier National Park, the largest single-peak glacier system in the U.S., Washington boasts more than 750 glaciers at North Cascades National Park.

No business like floe business. Most of Antarctica is a thick sheet of ice, where icebergs like giant's building blocks drop their miles-long bulk into the water. Along its edges, a wealth of marine mammals, fishes and birds live. Among them is the Weddell seal, foremost diver among pinnipeds, able to descend over 1,000 feet into the dark chill and return to chew breathing holes in the ice with its buck teeth.

surrounding terrain. These it deposits at its lower end, variously called the tongue, the toe, or the snout. Scientists call this point where the ice melts and drains off "the area of ablation." When the rate of accumulation equals the rate of ablation, the beginning and end points of the glacial conveyor belt stay in the same place as the glacier moves its load down the valley. This is how and why glaciers advance and retreat. Most glaciers today are retreating. But newsworthy exceptions exist. Hubbard Glacier in Alaska, for example, is known as a galloping glacier. Another

galloper – the Black Rapids Glacier south of Fairbanks, Alaska – made news in 1936-7. Geologists estimate its peak speed reached 200 feet a day. Within the last forty years, glaciers in India's Karakoram Range have surged down valleys at the phenomenal rate of 15 feet an hour!

Exploring glaciers is a bit like entering a dimension where everything you thought you knew about time and space gets blown away. From a distance you want to pick them up, turn these great curving swaths of ice over in your hands, examine the underbelly, trace crevasses and tunnels with your index finger, watch the meltwater run out. Up close, you can't even see the other end, let alone hold it. You see how your fragile human body could easily disappear into places in the ice where the summer sun has opened crevasses. You pick up a chunk of ice near the glacier's tongue with the realization that 200 years have passed since these crystals first fell as snow in some desolate high country. You squint your eyes westward and up, trying to take in the fact that the moon may have been rising over this icefield for three million years.

High in the accumulation zone, a glacier looks relatively smooth and sleek. The further you travel down the ice highway, the more like a bumpy back road it becomes. Although ice bends and stretches, it has its limits. Too much friction over irregular bedrock can cause the surface of the glacier to crack, forming crevasses more than 200 feet deep. People, dogs, sleds, and motorized ice vehicles can fall into these wicked wedge-shaped pits, making glacier travel hazardous. In Antarctica, the crevasses may be several miles long and 100 feet wide. The most spectacular crevasses occur at the tongue of the glacier. Glaciers may also be graced by icefalls. In places where the underlying bedrock drops sharply, the glacier "waterfalls" over a cliff, often crevassing in the process.

Although much glacial melt takes place at the tongue, ice along the surface of the glacier also turns to water. These meltwater streams, heaviest in the summer, have to go somewhere. In their search for low ground, they carve millwells and tunnels throughout the glacier. Nearly vertical, slick-sided, circular drains, millwells form when meltwater plunges into fractures and flows down shafts to emerge near the tongue. Geologists think that many of these tunnels form labyrinthine mazes, riddling the interior of the glacier with immense blue-violet caverns of frozen water.

The ablation zone at the tongue of the glacier looks the messiest. Here the glacier deposits much of its load, the pure white of distant snowfields now smudged and melted into a rocky road of brown rock and rubble.

Geologists classify glaciers by shape and position. An ice sheet is a flat or gentle slope covered with ice, fed entirely by snow falling directly on it. Because it rests on fairly level

An Arctic species, polar bears call the top of the world their domain. These well-padded, solitary carnivores prowl vast northern territories in Alaska, Canada, Greenland, Norway, and the Soviet Union, stalking seals and fish. Once hunted from aircraft, polar bears are now protected. Flightseeing from Canada or Alaska allows you to see them without endangering them. It's also a good way to grasp the almost-impossible grandeur of the far North, such as the nunatak peaks, right, that poke through the chilly meringue of the Juneau Ice field.

Glaciers possess a special sort of life. Born in high snowfields, they change, migrate, and grow old. And sometimes they give birth to icebergs, an ephemeral souvenir of themselves. This process, accompanied by rumbles, groans, and great splashes, is called calving. Most icebergs are offspring of tidal glaciers, whose tongues meet the sea. This particular tongue belongs to Grotto Glacier in Alaska's Wrangell-St. Elias National Park.

Not all the water in a glacier is locked up as ice. Meltwater streams flow from them, making spawning salmon and grizzly bears happy. Long, arcing waterfalls in Yosemite, Glacier, and North Cascades National Parks are also glacial handiwork. When smaller glaciers feed larger ones, their valley floors end up at different heights, like a split-level house. Centuries later, when the glaciers have retreated, hanging valleys graced with cascades are left.

uplands, the ice typically spreads out in all directions. If the ice is thick and heavy enough, the pressure can even shove it up a slope. Greenland and Antarctica are typical ice sheets. Smaller ice sheets may be called ice caps. The ice of vast sheets or caps may also escape from the upland plain by wearing gaps in the mountains. Tongues of ice escaping from broader ice sheets are termed outlet glaciers. They depend on the vast ice sheet for nourishment.

ther, more independent glaciers don't need constant nourishment from a mother ice field. Known as valley or alpine glaciers, they have their sources at the heads of their own high valleys. It isn't so much the constant buildup of snow that pushes alpine glaciers down their troughs; more often, it's the avalanching of snow from the steep slopes near the valley head. These glaciers gain their names from the form their troughs take. Cirque glaciers carve out a bowl in the side of a mountain, creating an amphitheater of ice. Cliff glaciers cling to small troughs on mountain faces. Piedmont glaciers fan out broad, flat masses of ice fed by higher-altitude valley glaciers. Tidal glaciers push their tongues all the way to the ocean's edge. Unlike massive ice fields where ice moves in any direction, including up, valley glaciers only descend.

Think of a glacier, and you imagine an awesome silence. Glaciers can make noise, however. In a process known as calving, a tidal glacier's tongue pushes icebergs into the sea. A tidal glacier's tongue normally rests in the water. The water's buoyancy causes the tongue to lift slightly, and brittle ice cracks along giant crevasses. Columns of ice then slide into the water. An iceberg may also calve if the seawater begins to melt the bottom portion of the tongue. Suddenly, the upper portion finds itself with no support and lets go of the ice wall, which plunges into the water below with the ponderous grace of a great blue whale. It makes a thunderous rumble of groans and a vast booming, then silence and the slow slap of swells as the great berg floats away.

Most of the icebergs in the Northern Hemisphere have broken off glaciers of the Greenland Ice Cap. Some of these giants have volumes of 50 cubic miles and tower 300 feet above the water. One of the largest bergs ever spotted by a disbelieving human was an Antarctic iceberg that measured 60 by 200 miles.

Large icebergs may wander for years, cruising through miles of ocean before melting. Because of their greater mass below water, they are a constant danger to ships. Four-fifths of an iceberg's height and seven-eighths of its mass lurk below the waterline. A giant berg littering a shipping lane caused the Titanic disaster in 1912. Small wonder that many nations spend big money on berg-detecting technology.

Icebergs pose hazards to smaller vessels, too. Kayaks or canoes venturing too close to calving glaciers or listing icebergs may be swamped by the swells they cause.

Not all bergs are king-size. Smaller chunks of ice called growlers or bergie bits often litter the water near a tidal glacier like shredded styrofoam. Larger than bergie bits but smaller than the monsters that calve from ice caps, most medium-sized icebergs last about a week. Slowly they float down the fjords towards the open sea, leaning and listing and melting as they go.

Polished rock, long scratches or striations, and boulders called erratics show where glaciers once scoured Yosemite Valley. Another left-behind is the pika, a rabbity Arctic species that migrated south with the glaciers and was stranded an eon or so ago. Its grass-eating companion species, the chirpy-voiced marmot, pictured at right, lives in alpine meadows.

Above water, the wind, rain, and sun work to release the inner art of the bergs. They constantly change, backsides rolling over to become tops, pinnacles melting, crevasses widening, bases worn by sloshing seawater. Creaking and groaning, they float by like old armchairs, trying to find a more comfortable position in the water.

We're not used to thinking of icebergs in color, but they do provide an astonishing variety. Their colors, along with their shapes and textures, result from the type of ice that forms them and where on the glacier they have been. Some are gray-brown, pock-marked messes, loaded with sticks and dirt, still carrying souvenirs of mountain peaks hundreds of miles away. From a kayak, you can watch the limb of an ancient spruce locked into the ice at hundreds of feet above sea level go floating by, while the unutterable cold of these cathedrals of ice bites into your face. The blue bergs seem especially chilly. Their ice is denser and coarser, a fibrous aqua blue. These bergs are often layered like schist, with walk-through crevasses wide enough to almost split the berg in two. The most ethereal icebergs have diamond fire. Their color – or lack of it – comes from trapped air bubbles locked in their icy crystals. They look like floating figurines, pinnacled sculptures with spires that curve and glisten, delicate and curved like an array of prisms hanging in your dining-room window.

Occasionally, icebergs get stranded by the tide on beaches. There they drip for the next few days, crystals wriggling and squeaking, rivulets like tiny alpine cascades sloshing out grooves, their wet flanks glistening. Their passing leaves huge dark paw-prints of moisture on the sand.

Moving sculptures of snow and ice themselves, glaciers also work over eons as landscape architects, to erode, transport, and ultimately, deposit.

A glacier erodes by rubbing its thick icy body against its trough for centuries. As it lumbers its icy way across centuries and down valleys, it acts as a giant rasp on the surrounding bedrock. Grinding down the valley floor, it tugs at rock fragments underneath and along its walls, pries boulders loose, plucks and chisels its way. Such movement causes scratches, called striations, in the underlying rock. You can pick up striated rocks and run your

★ **Best Glacier-gazing in the Northwest**

Explorers in the early 20th century endured much to reach the North and South Poles, to discover and name the glaciers and landmarks of the Arctic and Antarctic. Today's explorers find adventure in such feats as climbing the glaciers of Wyoming's Grand Tetons, and at far left, overcoming personal disabilities to traverse Ruth Glacier in Denali National Park, Alaska.

Map not to scale.

fingernail along these long gashes. A glacier may also enlist the help of the boulders it moves to etch surrounding rocks. A boulder being carried along the bottom of a glacier scrapes grooves in the underlying rock. This abrasive action works much like a slow-motion blender, grinding rock as fine as flour. Rock flour gives glacial streams their characteristic milky color and turns glacial lakes like Canada's Lake Louise a deep aqua blue.

Thousands of years of grinding eventually changes valley shapes. What may have started as a V-shaped stream valley gets hollowed out, its sides scraped off, its walls pushed back as the frozen tongue of ice descends. Typical glacial valleys become U-shaped troughs. In these valleys, high-altitude basins called cirques collect snow and hold it for centuries. Sometimes the weight of the snowpack and the pull of gravity will put a cirque glacier on the move. Cirques can move down toward the main glacier and chisel into the mountain as well. If a couple of cirques carve away side by side on a mountain peak, they leave between them a narrow, knife-edge ridge of rock called an arete. A lovely example is the Garden Wall arete in Montana's Glacier National Park. Peaks sometimes get gnawed at on all sides by cirques, ultimately making a pattern of aretes known as a horn. The most famous? Switzerland's Matterhorn.

Beauty within: an ice cave in the Muir Glacier remnant, Glacier Bay National Park, gleams like a sapphire. It was probably formed when meltwater streams at the glacier's surface tunneled their way into the interior. Ice caves can be explored in other spots such as Palisade Glacier in Mt. Rainier National Park.

What could be more daunting than the great glacial ice sheet of Antarctica? But penguins make Antarctica seem, if not hospitable, at least wondrous. Strangely enough, only two species call the South Pole home: the emperor and the Adélie penguin, pictured here, poised for an aquatic takeoff.

Glacial action also produces hanging valleys. When a main glacier carves out its U-shaped trough, the force of the ice deepens and broadens the valley at a faster rate than that of tributary glaciers. A small glacier feeding into a larger one will have a valley floor higher than the main valley. None of this is obvious when both valleys are full of ice. As the ice recedes, however, it exposes the difference. The smaller valley floor is often left dangling miles above the main valley floor. Streams that now drain these tributary valleys reach the lip of the hanging valley and cascade off its edge, sometimes falling thousands of feet. Bridal Veil Falls and other falls in California's Yosemite National Park are stunning examples. From the deeply cut fjords of Norway, Alaska, Iceland, Argentina, Chile, and Scotland to the picturesque Finger Lakes region of New York state, abandoned glacier valleys number among the world's most sublime sights.

Collectors of rocks, silt, and sand, glaciers move huge amounts of materials far from their origins. At some point, though, even a glacier gets tired and lets the load fall. By studying these curious glacial droppings, we can piece together the historical wanderings of glaciers.

Soil in much of the southern U.S., for instance, is typically weathered soil from the decomposed bedrock beneath it. In the north, however, much of the soil contains a mix of boulders, clay, sand, and gravel, often full of minerals not local to the area. When 19th century scientists finally accepted their Swiss colleague Louis Agassiz's theory of glaciation, they realized that much of this material had been scraped off territory far to the north and dragged south by glaciers.

The dumping follows characteristic patterns. As a glacier grinds down a valley, it pushes a pile of rock fragments pried from higher elevations. When the glacier pauses or retreats, whether seasonally or permanently, it leaves behind a long ridge where its tongue once was. Ridges marking the stops and starts of a glacier are called terminal moraines. A glacier may also create lateral moraines – piles of rubble that get caught and carried along the edges of the ice. Fresh moraines, such as the ones along Athabasca Glacier in Alberta, Canada, are sharp ridges of wasteland that rise over 400 feet. In spite of erosion, large glacial moraines still dot North America and north-central Europe. Portions of Cape Cod, Martha's Vineyard, Nantucket, and Long Island sit on 10,000-year-old moraines. Glacial rubbish may also be left as drumlins: inverted, teaspoon-shaped hills. Most drumlins measure about a mile long and can be 50 to 200 feet high. Boston's Beacon and Bunker Hills are perched on these glacial dumps.

A glacier also uses meltwater streams to flush

Believe it or not. Within sight of grazing zebra and other East African game sits Mt. Kilimanjaro, its dome crowned with an active glacier. At right, Mt. Cook and its glacier-rich companions make it apt to call New Zealand 'the Alps Down Under.' Glaciers even manage to hide within an active volcano at Katmai National Monument in Alaska's Aleutians.

its load. When a current runs out onto the plain, it slows and starts to deposit a mixture of rock waste called till. Layer after layer of till builds up in the plain, fanning away from the tongue. Because the layers are deposited unevenly, the streams change course, creating a braided pattern. Close to the glacier,

the heavier sand and gravel get dropped first. Farther away fall the silt and clay. In active outwash plains such as Athabasca Glacier, you can slog your way across quicksand-sticky silt and clay. The combination of meltwater action and the

slow retreat of melting glaciers has spread glacial till over much of the central U.S. and northern Europe. In places such as Iowa, it may lay in drifts 200 feet deep.

In the glacier's wild plundering, it often gouges out gigantic boulders. When the glacier retreats, these boulders, called erratics, are abandoned. Distinct from surrounding bedrock and unusually large, erratics have inspired legends all over the world. People once believed they were the handiwork of giants or devils. The Madison Boulder, one of the largest erratics ever found, squats on New Hampshire soil, a rocky lump 75 feet long, 35 feet wide, and 40 feet high. Erratics were often used to build castles, stone rings, and other religious or ceremonial structures. They may weigh over 100 tons and have been dragged over 800 miles from their original site.

Places of stark beauty, glaciers and icebergs may attract the artist, inspire the photographer, move the poet to marvel. But could living creatures inhabit such inhospitable places? Surprisingly, yes.

Some very small creatures spend their whole lives in or on the ice. The glacier flea, for instance, doesn't mind being frozen every night, stuck fast to the surface until daytime temperatures rise. Then he wanders over the surface of his slippery world, searching for a meal of conifer pollen that might have blown over the ice.

Although its most famous face, the Matterhorn, is a classic example of glacial carving, the Swiss Alps have hundreds of other glacial peaks, such as Shilthorn. By taking a cable car from the village below, glacier-gazers can take in a panorama and lunch from Shilthorn's 14,000-foot summit. Summer turns the Alps into a brilliant vertical garden of wildflowers, butterflies, and birds from the alpine hummer to the golden eagle.

The segmented glacier worm, on the other hand, lives its wriggly red life ice-bound. Snugged into air pockets within the glacier, this hardy one-inch creature feeds on red algae, diatoms, and bits of pollen it finds in its refrigerated home. Immobility doesn't guarantee safety, though. Ticks, mites, and snow buntings prey on it.

Most animals of the ice environment do not spend their lives encased. Rather, they live near the ice and use it to hunt, to migrate, to feed, to rest — even to hide. (Many furred and feathered creatures, from Arctic hares to ptarmigans, seasonally change color to blend better with ice and snow.)

Seals, sea lions, and walruses are great hitch-hikers, wiggling up onto large ice floes for transportation to new feeding grounds. Pinnipeds seem to enjoy basking on ice floes. By using their unfurred extremities to absorb heat, they help regulate body temperatures and conserve energy. The walrus is also able to increase its blood circulation by sunbathing, an adaption which turns its skin rich pink.

Certain species of seals recognize a good delivery room when they see it. They often birth their pups on icebergs or pack ice, surrounded by the moat of the ocean. This strategy isn't always 100 percent successful. Killer whales and Stellar sea lions, always on the alert for a seal meal, have been known to wash or bump seals, baby and all, off their bergs. Walruses and other pinnipeds use the isolation of icebergs for breeding activities also.

Wolves, polar bears, and Arctic foxes have long used the ice as moving sidewalks, hopping from floe to floe to patrol their immense territories throughout the Arctic year. Foxes prey on hares, seabirds, and lemmings, but will quite happily eat seal leftovers from polar bear meals. Polar bears hunt by waiting for seals to come up for air or out of their lairs. If no seals appear, a polar bear will go where the action is, swimming slowly but strongly for as much as 20 miles in the icy sea. Its fur-lined feet provide extra traction on the ice, giving it the ability to run on land at speeds up to 25 miles per hour. Other types of bears are not as at home in the severe terrain of glaciers. Grizzlies, for example, need a more varied habitat, and are more often found in areas where glaciers have receded. Once reputed to roam the glacial barrens, the glacial bear, a huge beast with a coat of steel-blue, is now thought to be a rare color phase of the black bear.

Many mammals use glaciers as frozen freeways. In glacial regions around the world, musk oxen, yaks, Tibetan antelopes, snow leopards, and ibex all migrate to feeding grounds by taking the direct route over glacier-covered mountain passes.

Come spring, the glacial habitat becomes a smorgasbord, an important feeding and breeding ground for a variety of species. Marmots and ground

Cottony dryas, often first to pioneer an area after a glacier retreats, helps anchor the soil. Later, stands of alder, hemlock, willow and spruce begin to root in the glacial rubble, providing habitat for bears, deer, and smaller animals. Pictured here are two areas of Glacier Bay in different stages of recovery.

More than a match for its chill environment, the Arctic fox wears a brown coat in summer, white or pale gray in winter. Blend-in colors help it hunt down hares, birds, and small mammals. As they roam the far north, Arctic foxes use glaciers as shortcuts and ice as stepping stones. The only time the fox takes shelter is to den large litters of cubs.

squirrels come out of hiberation. Ravens and snowy owls arrive to feast on lemmings and mice. Phalaropes gorge on insects. And a blizzard of other birds court, mate, nest, and produce young in the brief polar summer. Birds often take advantage of the ice to feed. Pipits and rosy finches find it easy to make a meal on the seeds which blow across glaciers. But it isn't just seeds they find. Insects, especially grasshoppers, have an unfortunate habit of getting stuck on the ice. Grasshopper Glacier near Yellowstone National Park is famous as the frozen fast-food section for wandering grizzlies and various birds. From an avian standpoint, icebergs are handy objects at any time. Bald eagles use pinnacle bergs as lookout towers. Cormorants adopt them as drying racks, holding out their wings as the berg drifts down a fjord. For gulls, albatrosses, kittiwakes, and other distance flyers, an iceberg represents an ideal resting spot on the way from here to there.

Snow can blush in Antarctica. In summer, red algae tints great stretches of snow and ice. This small living plant, a vital part of the polar food chain, gets nutrients from the snow. Its red pigment protects it from harmful ultraviolet rays.

Correctly or not, penguins may be the group of birds we most often associate with icebergs and glaciers. While it's true many of the 17 species prefer bracing cold, only two – the Adélie and the Emperor penguin – call Antarctica home. In early winter, the 90-pound emperor heads inland from the Antarctic ice shelves, nests, and lays its eggs. Then the male-female relay race begins. Once the egg is laid, the female hands off to the male, who obligingly stands still for two months, warming the egg in a fold of skin between his feet and stomach. She meanwhile spends two months in the sea, feeding on fish. Just before the chick is hatched, the female returns and the male leaves for his two-month turn at the dinner table. For months, these elegantly dressed, highly social birds, which cannot fly and can scarcely waddle on land, take turns standing guard on the ice, huddling for warmth.

Key player in the Antarctic food chain is krill, a tiny, shrimp-like organism. Superswarms of krill live in the seas around Antarctica, nourishing fishes, baleen whales, and many species in between.

qually tiny and humble plant species play key roles in the food chains of both polar regions. One recently discovered algae lives on the underside of pack ice. Another lives in ice and snow from the Alps to the Andes. A one-celled plant, it tints the snow red, pink or purple. The alga uses its flagellum, a tiny beating thread, to get into a comfortable position below the surface. There it spends its life, its modest needs fulfilled with a small quality of nutrients dissolved in the snow, its pigment filtering harmful ultraviolet light from the sun.

Longest locks in the animal world. Musk oxen thrive in the bitter cold of northern Alaska, Canada, and Greenland. Their thick coats, heavy horns, and habit of standing shoulder to shoulder in wagon-train formation conserve energy. Browsers by nature, musk oxen manage to find nourishment even in the unpromising plant growth of glacial regions. Herds of these buffalo look-alikes are now being re-established.

The glory of Alaska's Glacier Bay lies unfolded at 2000 feet. At this height, it is easy to appreciate the insistent flow of the glaciers to the sea, pushing their loads of rubble as they go.

Other plants have to wait until a glacier recedes and there is enough nourishment in the wasted moraines to support growth. Glacial till and outwash are low in nitrogen, so pioneer plants tend to be stunted and yellow. They specialize in survival, hugging the grounds to protect themselves from the constant wind and bitter cold. Yellow dryas are among the first plants to appear on recovering glacial outwash. Their creeping stems anchor them so they can search out nutrients in the soil. Their leaves also help build up the soil by catching wind-blown dust. River beauty, its rosy purple petals in stark contrast to the gray-brown drab of moraine, is another pioneer. Years later, bigger plants such as spruce, shrubby cinquefoil, and willow slowly creep closer, preferring at first the wrinkled shelter between the moraines. It takes several hundred years after a glacier has receded to build up enough soil for subalpine firs, heather meadows, and dense willow thickets.

While clues to the glaciers' stories are everywhere, actual glacier-gazing usually requires travel. In the United States, head for Montana, Washington, Wyoming, California, or best of all, Alaska. (See our maps on pages 17 and 38-39 for details.) In Canada, one of the most accessible glaciers in the world drains the Columbia Icefield near Jasper, Alberta. Here the Athabasca Glacier noses its way close to the Banff-Jasper Highway. In the summer you can easily hike onto the glacier itself. Much further south, in the Patagonian terrain between Argentina and Chile, Paine and Glacier National Parks give trekkers an array of peaks, penguins, and glaciers.

The Alps are where all the glacial theorizing started. Forming a backbone between

Mt. McKinley, North America's highest peak and the center-piece of Denali National Park, is great dogsled country. Although some Eskimos and Arctic tribes use traditional sled dogs, dwellings, and weapons, most have become dependent on the energy-wasteful methods of hunting and heating shown to them by whites. Unless all of us change our wasteful ways, time is running out for Alaska and other glacial ecosystems.

France, Italy, and Switzerland, the Alps bolt skyward. Glaciers and glacial traces abound. Further east, in the high mountain plateaus of Tibet and the Himalayas, the loftiest peaks on the planet are riddled with glaciers. Glaciers also carve their way through mountains in Norway, Sweden, New Zealand, and Iceland.

The last place you'd expect to find glaciers is along the equator. But they exist here, too. Small icy glaciers sprinkle the peaks of old Andes volcanoes sitting almost on top of the equator. In East Africa, glaciers ice the top of Mount Kilimanjaro. Summits in New Guinea towering thousands of feet above the South Pacific jungle sport numerous small glaciers. In fact, glaciers exist on every continent except Australia.

Scientists study glaciers to learn more about global weather, ocean currents, and how Ice Ages come and go. Not only do they want to find out about the past, they are anxious to learn what will happen next. We know that Pleistocene glaciation began less than one million years ago. During this era, four major Ice Ages occurred. When the

Pleistocene ended about 10,000 years ago, ice covered almost one-third of our planet. Today, about one-tenth of the land is hidden by ice. Scientists debate whether glaciers will once again grind their way down the country. Some believe the earth is beginning to cool again. Many others, however, point to the biggest unknown in the equation – human beings. Our burning of hydrocarbon fuels affects world climate to an as-yet unknown extent. Glacial ice is yielding some of the most ominous clues to a warming planet. Scientists are now able to analyze the quality of air trapped in the bubbles of glacial ice hundreds of years old. In it, they have found much lower levels of atmospheric carbon dioxide. Today's rising levels of this gas produced from burning fossil fuels add to the greenhouse effect. A warmer planet means melting polar ice caps. How serious would this be? Well, 75% of the fresh water in the world is locked up in ice – and 99% of this ice is in Antarctica. A one- to two-foot rise in the sea level from melting ice would drown coastal cities worldwide.

Perhaps the most tantalizing quality that glaciers hold is the ubiquity of their clues. Whether you vacation in the Finger Lakes, farm the deep glacial till of Iowa, climb El Capitan in Yosemite, or kayak the southeast coast of Alaska, their fingerprints are everywhere. They remind us that we are parts of larger stories that stretch to other places and times. Standing at the toe of a glacial wall towering hundreds of feet above your head, you pull your scarf against the glacial winds and feel yourself shrinking, your concept of time collapsing like a cold white filament. You are reminded that something much larger than us has worked this land for thousands of years.

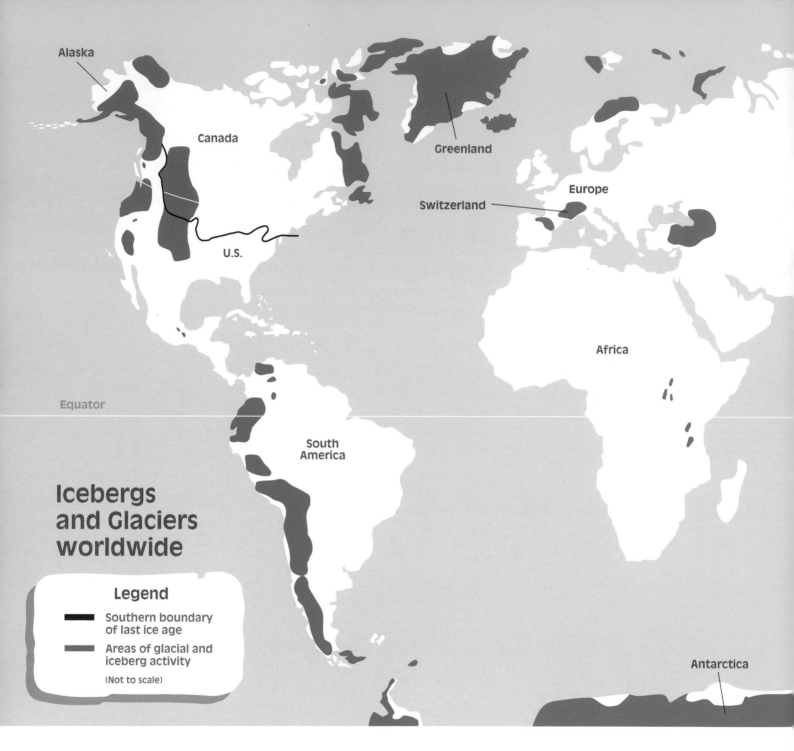

Icebergs and Glaciers worldwide

Alaska

Canada

Greenland

Europe

Switzerland

U.S.

Africa

Equator

South America

Legend

Southern boundary of last ice age

Areas of glacial and iceberg activity

(Not to scale)

Antarctica

Where to see icebergs and glaciers

With 200,000 active glaciers around the globe, great glacier-gazing is possible almost anywhere.

Alaska: Some glaciers can be driven to or skiied, such as those on Mt. McKinley, others reached by flightseeing, but the best way to see Alaska's tidal glaciers is on the water. Cruise ships and smaller vessels regularly call at Glacier Bay, Prince William Sound, College Fjord, around Juneau, and at Yakutat Bay near Wrangell-St. Elias National Park. Kayaking, sailing in many of these areas. **Washington:** North Cascades, Mt. Rainier, and Olympia National Parks offer hundreds of glaciers and scenic

pluses. **California:** small active glaciers plus spectacular glacial traces in Yosemite National Park and nearby Devils Postpile. **Montana:** At Glacier National Park, famous Going-to-the-Sun Road, 60 active glaciers, many hanging valleys. **Wyoming:** Grand Teton National Park, a favorite with climbers. **Colorado:** Rocky Mountain National Park has Iceberg Lake, hiking to glaciers. **Canada and Greenland:** Mt. Robson Provincial Park in B.C.; Wrangell Mountains in Yukon; Banff and Jasper National Parks in Alberta; the Northwest Territories and Newfoundland. Greenland is full of active glaciers, and huge icebergs. **South America and Antarctica:** Glacier-clad peaks throughout the Andes from Ecuador to Chile, but the finest trekking and viewing is in Paine

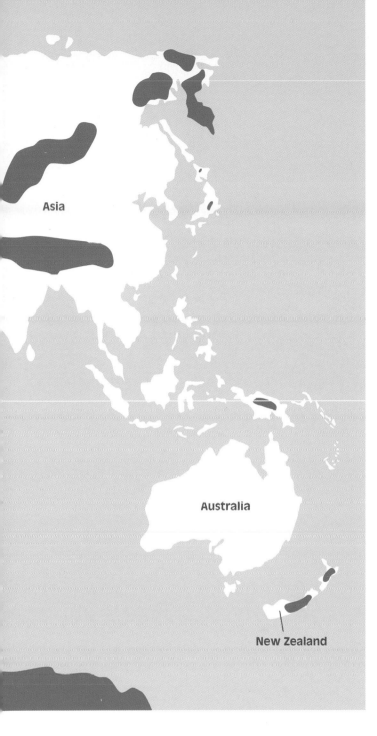

Asia

Australia

New Zealand

National Park in Chile, and Glacier or Fitzroy National Park in the Patagonian region of Argentina. Far-flung but well worth the trouble and expense are Antarctica and its associated islands. **Europe and Asia:** Norway, Vatnajokull Ice Cap of Iceland, Pyrenees glaciers in Spain, Turkey. In the Alps, the Glacier Express train winds through Switzerland for 150 miles from St. Moritz to Zermatt. The three great mountain ranges of Asia – Himalayas, the Hindu Kush, and Karakoram – located in Nepal, Tibet, India, and Pakistan, offer magnificent glaciers and trekking. **Oceania:** The Southern Alps of New Zealand are very popular with mountaineering groups. **Africa:** several glaciers over the 17,000-foot level; Kenya's Mt. Kilimanjaro is the most interesting.

Special Thanks

Don and Carol Hurd; Joanne Main and Tintype Graphic Arts; Samuel Matthews and Elizabeth Manierre at National Geographic; Kari Glass and Joel Curtis; Archie Hanson; Dick Blake. Maps on pages 17, 38-39 and illustrations on pages 8, 13, 24, and 29 designed by David Butz.

About the Author

Barbara Wilson lives in Frostburg, Maryland. A poet and non-fiction writer, her work has appeared in *Sierra, Three Rivers Poetry, Stone Country, Southern Poetry Review* and elsewhere.

About the Photographers

A major contributor to this book is **Art Wolfe**, internationally known for his striking animal portraits and natural landscapes. Beginning with the cover, Art's photos can be found on pages 20-21, 22-23, 30-31, 32, 33, and 34-35.

The other photographers who made this book a superb photo essay:

Tom Bean/DRK Photo: pages 10-11, 18-19
Ralph A. Clevenger: pages 4, 24
Ken Cole/Animals Animals: page 37
Jeff Foott: page 16, upper photo
John Fowler: page 16, lower photo
François Gohier: pages 27, 28
Richard Hansen: page 14, lower photo
Fred Hirschmann: pages 2-3, 5, 9
Frans Lanting/Minden Pictures: inside front cover, all photos pages 6-7
Brian P. Lawler: 2 photos on page 26, page 40
Tom Mangelsen: back cover, page 8
Kevin Schafer: pages 14-15, upper photo
Twila Stofer: page 25
Tim Thompson: pages 29, 36
Larry Ulrich/DRK Photo: page 12
Kennan Ward: page 13, inside back cover

Recommended Reading

Glacier by Ronald H. Bailey (Time-Life Books, 1982)
Last Places by Lawrence Millman (Houghton Mifflin,1990)
Arctic Dreams by Barry Lopez (Scribner,1986)
National Geographic issues: 1/87, 1/84, 2/83

"To approach and touch these white monsters that have been carving mountains for thousands of years is a bit eerie — like running your fingers over the face of a god who doesn't flinch."

— Barbara Wilson